Beating Debt & Building Wealth

A Financial Guide for Christians

The borrower is a slave to the lender—Proverbs 22:7

ISBN: 1-4033-9839-9 (e-book)
ISBN: 1-4033-9840-2 (Paperback)

This book is printed on acid free paper.

1stBooks – rev. 01/03/03

Acknowledgements

First and foremost I would like to thank my father in heaven, for without him where would I be. Next I would like to acknowledge and thank the three women in my life. First to my soul mate and partner in life, my wife Carrie whose encouragement and support have made me the man I am today. Second to my always-loving mother Mary, your guidance has kept me straight. Third to my "Ladybug" Corrie, my reason for living and fighting everyday. Others that I would like to acknowledge include my Co-founder and brother Amos Reese, my spiritual counselor pastor Ricky L. Campbell as well as family and friends

Beating Debt & Building Wealth

A Financial Boot-Camp for Christians

The borrower is a slave to the lender—Proverbs 22:7

During the last 50 years nothing in the area of finances has dominated or influenced the direction of our society as much as debt. It's amazing when you consider that only a generation ago credit cards were unknown, car loans were a rarity, and mortgages were for GIs who were getting starter homes. But today it is not unusual for a young couple to owe—with home mortgages, school loans, and car loans—$100,000 or more within the first two years of marriage. Although this has become the norm in our society, is it NOT the norm according to God's principles of finance?

Becoming debt free

With the desire, discipline, and time, anyone can become debt free and stay that way. There are five basic steps to debt elimination: (1) Transfer ownership of every possession to God; (2) Give the Lord His part first—the tithe on gross income; (3) Develop a realistic balanced budget that will allow every creditor to receive as much as possible; and (4) Reduce and eliminate all debt (no bank or family loans and cut up the credit cards); (5) Give. Generally speaking, if these steps are followed, the average family will be debt free in less than five years.

Congratulations! By participating in the Beating Debt...and Building Wealth seminar, you are taking a major step toward your financial freedom. It is our sincere wish that the techniques and strategies you'll learn in this program would help you over come the bondage of debt and build a bright and prosperous future.

Lonnie R. Mathews
Co-founder

Amos F. Reese
Co-founder

TABLE OF CONTENTS

INTRODUCTION

If you've ever taken kids shopping you know they usually see lots of things that they "want" but you seldom hear the word "want" as they beg, and plead. More often it's "I NEED I NEED."

Even as adults, some of us have trouble distinguishing between life's needs and wants. With easy access to credit we often spend more than we can afford. So we end up borrowing, and then repaying the money with interest. Whether we take out a loan or charge expenses on a credit card, borrowing ties up future money and costs us the compound interest we might have earned if we had invested the money instead.

Consider This:

According to CardWeb.com, the average US household carried credit card balances of nearly $8,000 in 2000. If the interest rate were 19%, annual interest payments alone would have amounted to $1,520. Now consider what might have happened if that $1,520 was invested each year in your company's tax-deferred retirement savings plan. Over a 20-year period, at an 8% average annual rate of return, your investment has the potential to grow to $69,558.19. With a company match, your nest egg could potentially be even greater.

Regaining control of your financial situation takes hard work, perseverance, planning and most of all, self-discipline but in the end it allows you to move toward a more secure financial future. When we continue to use debt to finance our wants and desires we are assuming that God is going to continue to bless us, but in reality we don't know if we will continue to be blessed *"Do not boast about tomorrow, for you do not know what a day may bring forth"*—Proverbs 27:1. We can and will not ever know when the test will come. In today's economy you are subject to get laid-off, what would that do to your financial situation?

The use of debt is slowly destroying lives; last year over 850,000 individuals filed bankruptcy. Families are spending more and more of their personal income on debt reduction. In fact, a recent study revealed that consumers spend one out of every five dollars in take-home pay on personal debts, not including home mortgages. 56 percent of all divorces are a result of financial tension in the home. Now day's marriage vows should be *"till DEBT do us part."*

It may or may not surprise you to learn how much the Bible says about money and finances. In fact, there are more than 2,300 bible verses on money and how we should us it in our lives. Jesus Christ himself said more about money than any other subject.

THE PROBLEM

Today we live in a society that believes that debt is normal *"why wait...when I can buy it now and pay later"*. Often individuals lose sight of the big picture when buying things on credit that is until they are confronted with massive credit card debt. When you look at the statistics of individuals and the debt that has developed, the average American spends $1.10 for every dollar they earn.

- The average household has **4** credit cards with balances around $8,000 up from two cards and $2,340 five years ago.

- Credit card companies set their minimum payments at 2% of the outstanding balance or $10 per month

- Only 2% of Christians tithe covering 80% of the financial responsibility of the church.

- More than 70 % of all consumers live from **paycheck to paycheck**

- USA Today reports that 30% of Americans have less than $15,000 saved for retirement

What is debt? Webster defines debt as money or property which one person is obligated to pay to another. Nothing good can come from the "buy now and paying later" attitude. Advertisers are consistently bombarding consumers with ads that promise the good life. We are lead to believe that we should go out and buy their products no matter what you have to do to get them, even if it means borrowing to get them.

What does it really cost when you use debt?

Debt has a much higher cost than you realize. The next time you are tempted to use debt think of what it really cost. For instance if you purchase a couch for $1,000 at 13%, just making the minimum payment it would take you 12 years to pay back the $1,000 plus and additional $815 in interest. Debt is a cancer slowly eating away at society. Debt takes a physical as well as a financial toll on individuals. The stress associated with having to make payments contributes to mental and emotional fatigue. Debt ruins relationships; the most important relationship of all is our relationship with God.

When we are in debt it is difficult to focus on God and what he has planned for our lives. God's view on debt is *"Owe no man anything except to love one another: for he that loveth another hath fufilled the law."* –Roman 13:8. The bible is very clear on debt, in fact nowhere in the bible is it mentioned that we should use debt for anything. When we are in debt we are distracted from the works of the kingdom. When we are in debt we are in a position of servitude, *"The rich ruleth over the poor, and the borrower is slave to the lender."* –Proverbs 22:7

The deeper you are in debt the less freedom you have to serve God. You don't have full freedom to decide where to spend the income that you have been blessed to earn, your income has been legally obligated to others. God does not have a problem with Christians having money, just as long as it doesn't interfere with our relationship with him. Think how difficult it is to truly focus all of your energy on God and doing his work when you are burdened down with debt. How many times have you been in church, and all you can think about is your financial situation. How many times have you wanted to give the tithe, but just couldn't. God's word says that as Christians we will receive financial blessings if we are committed to him. So why is it that there are so many Christians who love the Lord with all their hearts struggling to live from check to check?

MONEY AND GOD

Money is important to God; it can be a powerful tool in the hands of faithful Christians. Myths and religious traditions have been keeping many of us confused regarding our economic destiny. Many have been programmed by these myths and traditions to have the wrong attitude about money. *"All to well you reject the commandment of God, that you may keep your tradition."* –Mark 7:9 It seems as though there has been a steady flow of partial truths and mixed distortions to keep us confused in the area of proper money management. Some of the more common myths about God and money are:

1. GOD IS NOT CONCERNED ABOUT MONEY

Nothing could be further from the truth, the scriptures contain over 700 direct references about money— including two-thirds of the parables and one out of every six verses in the Gospels concern themselves with the right and wrong use of material possessions. God has and will continue to use money in scriptures to help lead our path for he knows that which is close to our heart will lead us astray *"So you ought to have deposited my money with the bankers, and at my coming I would have received back my own with interest."* –Matthew 25:27

2. MONEY IS THE ROOT OF ALL EVIL

The principle brought forth in the scriptures is that the love of money is "is the root of all evil" [1 Tim 6: 9-10]. This is one of the most misread scriptures about money, it is the love of money that corrupts any individual not money itself... money, in and of itself, is neither virtuous nor evil. In other words money is not to rule us—Christ is to be our ruler. However, how we handle money will reveal our true priorities and our faithfulness in what God gives us.

3. *YOU MUST REMAIN POOR TO FOLLOW JESUS*

Jesus told the young ruler to sell his possessions and give his money away [Luke 18:18-22]; therefore if you love Jesus and want to serve him you should take a vow of poverty. You will obtain true riches when you get to heaven. In this verse Jesus told the young ruler to sell his possessions and follow him because Jesus knew that the rulers heart was on his possessions. Christians do not have to be poor to get to heaven.

4. *HAVING A SAVINGS SHOWS A LACK OF FAITH IN GOD*

You should not hoard up money [Matt. 6:19]; therefore you should not have surplus or savings accounts. Having bank accounts limits your trust in God. Again, God wants our heart not our treasures. You can have your wealth on earth just don't let your treasures take your focus from God.

At the core of every myth is a distorted biblical principle. Many of our attitudes about God's provisions are distorted because of misinformation. On the surface, these fables may sound humorous or even very religious. Yet, even though none of the above myths are true, they grip the hearts and souls of Christians and non-Christians alike. Somehow these very traditions have been responsible for robbing us of our economic inheritance. As believing Christians we must be careful not to let myths and traditions keep us from receiving God's true blessings. God warns his people about the information that we receive. *"Beware of false prophets, who come to you in sheep's clothing, but inwardly they are ravenous wolves."* –Matthew 7:15

4

THE PLAN

Just as God uses money in our lives to lead our paths, the devil also uses money to shackle us and get us off track. It is important for Christians to understand the dangers of poor money management and financial bondage.

In earlier times being in debt meant physical bondage. In the past, if you found yourself not able to pay your debt then you were an indentured servant to the person that you owed. Worse yet you could find your self-thrown in to debtors' prison. God warns us about being in debt, *"the borrower is a slave to the lender"*—**Proverbs 22:7** Debtor's prison no longer exists at least from a physical standpoint, but it is replaced by mental anguish. It is not just the lack of money, but also the abundance of money that results in mental anguish if there is too much money, and then you worry about losing it. It is your attitude about money that God is concerned about.

Why Plan?

Often times Christians question whether or not to plan for the future. Planning is essential to success in any situation but especially in financial planning. God says *"For which one of you, when he wants to build a tower; does not first sit down and calculate the cost to see if he has enough to complete it?"*—Luke 14:28

Often times in our lives we plan for those things that are important to us. Imagine having a wedding and no one planned anything; it is safe to say that this event would be a disaster. When it comes to our financial lives we seldom plan how our finances will be spent. We automatically assume that we will always be able to earn income.

The average household income in America is somewhere around $40,000 per year. When asked 80 percent of those surveyed said that they have not planned how they are going to spend next years income.

Think about it, an individual or family that makes $40,000 per year, would have made $160,000 in four years time. Do this, think of your annual income now multiply that number by four. Now that you have that figure in mind, ask yourself how is my life going to be changed in the next four years.

—For better or For worse—

THE BONDAGE OF DEBT

The seed of bad financial management is planted early in our lives, honestly we were never taught about sound money management as children and consequently we end up bad money managers as adults. Many of us are but a disaster away from financial ruin. Have you ever thought *"what would I do if I lost my job tomorrow, how would my family and me live"?* The sad truth is that this is what it takes for many of us to realize that there is a problem, and that problem is DEBT. Many Christians today are shackled by excessive debts, and the misuse of

> *Do not be one of those who shake hands in a pledge, One of those who is surety for debts* **—Proverbs 22:26**

finances has ruined our spiritual lives. We are no longer able to minister to people as God directs because we are distracted by our own personal financial situation. When debt gets out of control it can render us useless to the kingdom of God. Debt becomes your master and not God.

The first step to becoming free from financial bondage is to learn how to develop a surplus. This process is easy; all you have to do is **SPEND LESS THAN YOU MAKE!!** If you spend less than you make then you will have a surplus, and it is from the surplus that you can do greater works in the Kingdom of God. The next few pages will reveal how you can get out of debt and stay debt free.

Release from Servitude

With the desire, discipline, self-control and commitment anyone can become debt free and stay that way. You and only you must take responsibility for your financial situation. Stop using excuses and being the victim take charge of your finances. If financial freedom is your priority then every dollar that you have after your basic needs have been met must go toward debt reduction. If that is true then over time your real priorities will surface and your less important wants and desires will fade. It is our belief at Alliance Financial Ministries that to become debt free there are five basic steps to debt elimination: (1) Transfer ownership of every possession to God; (2) Give the Lord His part first—the tithe on gross income; (3) Develop a realistic plan. A balanced budget will allow every creditor to receive as much as possible; (4) Reduce and eliminate all debt (no bank or family loans and cut up the credit cards); and (5) Give. Generally speaking, if these steps are followed, the average family will be debt free in less than five years. When we submit our lives to Jesus Christ, we must place high value on the importance of obedience. Read Romans 13:5-10 and assess your financial situation. What is God saying to you? Is debt causing damage to your walk with Him? If so, begin to pray about a solution. God will be faithful when you reach out for His help to achieve freedom from the bondage of debt. One of the greatest strongholds the enemy has on a Christian is money. Christians are constantly under pressure to keep up with the "Joneses". Advertisers tell us that we must satisfy our wants and desires, and some how we believe that by satisfying these cravings and desires will bring us happiness.

1. <u>Transfer ownership</u>

The first step to debt freedom is to pray and ask for the Lord's help and guidance. Then in prayer transfer ownership of each and every possession to Him. That means money, job, time, material possessions, family, education, and future earning potential. This is a mandatory first step. Failure to comply with this first step means that the events affecting any possession are sure to affect your attitude towards God. God does not

> *"Everything in the heavens and earth is yours, O Lord, and this is your Kingdom. We adore you as being in control of everything. Riches and honor come from you alone, and you are the Ruler of all mankind; your hand control power and might and it is at your desecration that men are made great and given strength"*
> **–I Chronicles 29:11-12**

force His will on anyone; therefore, you must willingly surrender your will and possessions to God. Without this all-important step of genuine acceptance that God is the owner of everything, Christians will never have financial freedom.

Without transfer of ownership and the right attitude; the poor will continue to struggle for improvement; the middle class will continue to transfer their wealth to creditors by borrowing; and the wealthy families will put their trust in their riches and not GOD. From the beginning we were bought with a price, and we are not our own. When we refuse God's ownership, it takes us out of his will. Once we transfer ownership that doesn't mean we sit and wait for something to happen, it simply means that we have matured and are ready to except God's plan for our finances. It means that we are now willing to do our part.

2. <u>**Establish the tithe**</u> *(Malachi 3:10)*

Once ownership of all possessions has been transferred to God, giving Him the first part, the tithe of gross income, will be the next step. Withholding the tithe from God indicates that ownership has not been transferred, therefore denying him the opportunity to bring his power into full focus with regard to our finances. If God is given the freedom to work unobstructed on behalf of our finances—by giving Him the tithe of our first fruits—He can give us his best. Somewhere in our culture tithing has become an issue of great debate and speculation. The bible gives several scriptures to decide how to tithe. As believing Christians, we have to first accept the word of God as the gospel meaning; we cannot pick and chose which part of the bible to obey. Having said that, the Old Testament is just as important as the New Testament. *II Timothy 3:16*

God evaluates our hearts concerning giving. When we give we direct our attention and heart to God. The concept of tithing is very clear: to keep God first in our lives. For example, what we do

> *"If therefore ye have not been faithful in the unrighteous mammon (money), who will commit to your trust the true riches?"* **—Matthew 16:11**

with our money first shows where our heart is. Giving God the first part of our check immediately focuses our heart and attention on him. Tithing also reminds us that all we have and will have belongs to God. Regular tithing continuously keeps God as the top priority in our lives and helps give proper perspective on everything else in our lives. We must remember that blessings come from God and are not always material and may not be experienced completely here on earth. When we give we should do so with anticipation that God will continue to provide our needs.

3. Develop a realistic budget *(Luke 14:28)*

When it comes to budgeting many have tried and failed. To master the budget, a successful budget will have the following features that are necessary for success.

- **A budget must be written**

To accurately know where your money is going you have to write it down. It does not matter how good you are with numbers, you must sit down and spend every dollar of your income on paper in advance.

- **Everyone must be involved**

The family that **Prays** together stays together. The same principle applies to financial success; everyone that is involved in the household finances must participate in the budget. It is extremely difficult if not impossible to successfully live on a budget if every family member is not actively involved. It is especially important for both husband and wife to AGREE as to how the family finances are spent.

- **Must be done regularly and in advance**

A budget is nothing more than a spending plan. To plan is to act in advance of an event. To budget is to spend future dollars before they arrive. It does not matter if you use sophisticated software or a note pad and pencil; you must spend next month's earnings before next month arrives. The more this is done the easier it becomes.

- **Keep it simple silly (KISS)**

The concept of budgeting should be kept simple. Next month's income should be more than next month's expenses, in other words SPEND LESS THAN YOU MAKE! Once you have spent next month's income on paper you must track you results and compare them to your plan, make any adjustments as necessary.

Budgeting made simple

For which of you, intending to build a tower, does not sit down first and count the cost, whether he has enough to finish it –Luke 14:28

An important part of achieving financial freedom is to live within your means, in other words spend less than you make on a regular basis. This part of the road to financial freedom will require changes in several areas of your life; the first change is with your attitude, someone once said, "The definition of a fool is to doing the same thing over and over and expecting a different result". When forming your spending plan you must keep in mind that generally you're spending falls into three main categories. Money will be spent in order of **NEEDS, WANTS**, and **DESIRES.**

NEEDS – these are the items that you would purchase to provide your basic necessities. Things like food, shelter, clothing, insurance etc… Our natural instinct would be to take care of this category first. One of the biggest problems with Christians these days is discerning what a true need is. I can't tell you how many times I have heard my wife say, "I think we need" when in actuality we don't really need a new entertainment center for the game room. We must first be able to understand our true needs.
Generally, your needs will take up the largest portion of your budget. Commit your needs to God and be obedient to his word *"If you have food and covering, with these we shall be content"* – *1 Timothy 6:8*

WANTS – the next category involves the choices we make about the quality of goods that we purchase. There is nothing inherently wrong with wanting nice things. The problem comes when we confuse wants with needs, this could be the difference between hamburger vs steak, designer clothes vs plain clothes or a new car vs a used car. A lot of problems come when we want too much to soon and sometimes that means going into debt to get it. It is important to keep things in perspective when it comes to deciding needs verses wants. *"But let it be the hidden person of the heart with the imperishable quality of a gentle and quiet spirit which is precious in the sight of God" —1 Peter 3:4*

DESIRES – To spend money on desires is to spend money after all of your needs and wants have been met. These should be your long-term goals; you should pray to God and ask that your desires be met. Examples of desires are world travel, new luxury vehicles etc… It is important that God has intervened because God has warned that our focus should be on heavenly things and not worldly goods. *"Do not love the world or the things in the world. If anyone loves the world, the love of the father is not in him." – 1 John 2:15*

Developing a proper spending plan requires several logical and sequential steps. The form used to continue this process is the Income and Expense Form; this form will assist in the allocation of your income into various categories. When you finish this form, you will find out one of two things either you have excess income or more expenses than income. Either way you will have to come up with a plan to address the situation at hand. I must warn you that once you have completed the income and expense form the results can be shocking for many and not so shocking for others. We have found that most individuals can just about figure out where the problems lie, and others are just in denial that there is a problem. The income and expense form makes this all clear.

Completing the I&E form is relativity simple in concept however, difficult to do in reality. Just when you think you have accounted for everything in all the categories something new comes up. It may take several tries to come up with a final spending plan. The first step is to list income from all sources including **GROSS** salary from your employer. Now that you have listed all of your income you have a basis to start, next subtract 10% of that amount for tithes to the Lord and any other taxes that are applicable. Once you have subtracted the tithes and taxes you have the Maximum Spendable Income.

This is the most you have available to spend on all three major categories *Needs, Wants,* and *Desires.* You should make it a point to live on less than this amount, what you may find is that you have been living above this amount and it has caused you to feel like you are in a financial pinch. More than likely you will realize that you are spending too much in one category or another and an adjustment needs to be made. If for example, if you are currently receiving child support and there's a possibility that you will not be able to count on it, then don't include that amount. Now that you have your Maximum Spendable Income *(MSI)*, you must divide it into the different categories.

Housing (36% of MSI)*
Typically, this is going to be the one of if not the largest expense in your budget. This may even be a problem in most budgets. Sometimes individuals purchase too much house for their budget. There are many reasons why people end up buying too much house, perhaps peer pressure or some other motivator. None the less your home should not take up more than 36% of your MSI that is to include all the expenses associated with owning a home Mortgage, Insurance, Taxes, Utilities and Maintenance. This could be difficult for some individuals to understand, this might mean that you should get a smaller house than you want or reduce your cable bill. Therefore the decision to purchase a home should be based on your true need and financial ability to keep and maintain a home and not some other outside source. To calculate utility payments that change from month to month, figure an average payment by adding the highest months and dividing by three, this will give you a rough estimate of your utility bills.

Food (12% of MSI)
The food portion of your budget should be monitored very carefully because many families typically purchase too much or too little food. Too much food means that food will go to waste, and too little food means that families eat out more. Either way both cases will destroy your budget. To reduce your food bill, you must watch the quality and the quantity of the food you buy. The total food bill should not consume more than 12% of your maximum spendable income. These amounts will vary of course depending on the size of your family. This portion of your budget includes all the food and beverages you buy at the grocery store, this includes any pet food but it does not include take-out or eating outside of the home. This type of food will be discussed in a later section.

Automobiles (15% of MSI)

The second biggest purchase that a family will make is that of an automobile. By and large, a car is the major problem area for most people especially the purchase of a brand new vehicle. I am famous for saying that *"a car is a worthless investment –Why because it is WORTH-LESS every year that you own it."* With that in mind, why would anyone waste his or her time and hard earned cash on a new vehicle? The sad truth is many families only keep their cars about four years, only to get suckered into a new one. Automobiles should take up about 15% of your MSI, which is to include the actual car payment, insurance, maintenance and taxes. Unfortunately most families buy a car that they cannot afford, which causes other areas of their budget to suffer. If this is your case it is not the end of the world, but you must be aware of this and make the necessary adjustments. This could mean selling your new car for a reliable used vehicle.

Insurance (5% of MSI)

Insurance is one area that many families are misled in. Very few individuals understand insurance, what kind or how much is needed. Insurance should not take up more than 5% or your MSI. Insurance should be used to supplement the income of an individual if they were no longer able to provide that income, either through disability or death. Insurance should not however be used for anything else such as a retirement savings.

Debts (5% of MSI)

Credit cards, bank loans, and installment credit are all fleecing America one month at a time. Lavish living through the use of credit has cause many families to go deeply into debt. This style of living and having to make payments has caused American families to spend more than the recommended 5% of their Maximum Spendable Income on debt payments. This is another area that destroys a budget. To feel at the least comfortable about your situation, the total of all your minimum payments should not be more than 5% of your income. However in most cases this number is a lot higher than the allotted 5%. You must work very hard to clear this up, take a few moments and look at the actual dollar amount. Now, think for a minute how your life would change if you didn't have to pay this amount. Imagine if you saved or invested this amount over the next three to five years.

Medical Expenses (4% of MSI)
Illnesses are part of life; and you must anticipate these expenses in your budget and be prepared for their cost. It is important that you set aside a small amount of your MSI *(approximately 4%)* for unexpected doctor visits and prescriptions.

Miscellaneous Expenses (5% of MSI)
This category includes everything not listed in all the other categories such as health and beauty aids, haircuts and cleaning supplies, laundry soap and other expenses. To calculate the cost of theses products or services all you have to do is divide the cost of the products by the number of months between purchases.

See table below

Item	Cost	How often purchased	Monthly Amt.
Bath soap	$4.00	6 bar / two months	$2.00
Haircut	$10.00	Every month	$10.00
Laundry soap	$5.00	Every three months	$1.66
Toothpaste	$2.50	Every other month	$1.25
		Total Monthly Misc.	**$14.91**

Once you have an idea of what each miscellaneous item cost you per month then add then up. Next, put that total on the I&E form.

Entertainment (7%)
Depending on your income and the amount you are already spending on other categories you may not have very much money left for this category. Sometimes too much entertainment could be the problem area in your budget. This category should not be more than 7% of your MSI. This includes eating out and any other form of entertainment, items such as movies *(rental or theater)*.

There has been much discussion of whether cable TV falls into this section; some argue that cable TV is a household item. What it really comes down to is personal choice. Other items included are sporting events, concerts and vacation. If you go on vacation only once a year, divide the amount you spend by 12. If you go to events only once in a while, figure how much you spend each year and divide that by 12 as well. Once you have figured out all of your entertainment expense add them up and put that amount on the entertainment line of the Income and Expense form.

Savings (5%)
As difficult as it may seem, it is very important that some sort of savings be established. In most cases, it is the lack of savings that makes credit use a lifelong way of life. When there is no savings and small emergencies happen like auto repairs, minor household repairs, medical expenses etc. you are forced to continue to use credit. A minimum of 5% of your MSI should be directed to a saving plan. If saving is difficult for you consider an automatic withdrawal from your checking account. A savings account can easily and effectively replace the "Emergency" Credit Card.

Childcare / School expenses (6%)
A large segment of society is a dual income family. Childcare expenses can cause an extra category in an already tight budget. If you find yourself having to pay for this expense then you must subtract monies from other areas of your budget to meet this expense. It is really difficult to measure how much should be spent on quality childcare. Generally 6% of your MSI is a good measuring point.

Traditionally, the idea of a budget has negative connotations associated with it. However, a budget is the exact opposite. Think of a budget as a spending plan where you are deciding what you are going to spend your income on before you receive it. YOU make the choice where your money is spent based on the priorities YOU set. A budget needs to be a written plan that allocates percentages of your Maximum Spendable Income (MSI) into different living expense categories, and there must be strict adherence to the budget. The use of a budget is a positive and empowering tool.

One of the most invigorating feelings you will ever have is when you have transitioned from living from paycheck to paycheck and living on a budget. The first two or three months the budget may not work, this is normal because there are always expenses that you did not anticipate. Make the necessary adjustments and keep trying. A budget will take a lot of pressure off you as you spend your income every month before it arrives. Imagine the feeling that on the first of every month you know exactly what bills you are going to pay and when those bills come in you simply pay them. Remember the budget is a very important weapon in the battle to gain control of your personal finances.

4. <u>Reduce and eliminate all debt</u>

70% of all American families live paycheck to paycheck and have practically no savings. The truth is we are programmed to think that debt is normal. Today, debt is the most aggressively marketed product available. Consumer debt increased by 25% from 1991 to 2001. Revolving credit card debt has climbed by 30% during same period. The biggest obstacle to reducing and ultimately eliminating debt is breaking the cycle of credit card use. In other countries consumer saving rates can be as high as 15%, while in the US the average savings rate is below 0%. To save is not a matter of spirituality nor does it represents a lack of faith. You merely need cash available for those unexpected emergencies. Our research has shown that it is not the day to day living that keeps Christian in debt; it is the unplanned expenses that come up from time to time. When we do not have cash available to take care of those unexpected expenses, instead of relying on provisions from God we use credit.

The only way to accumulate no additional debt is to cut up existing credit cards and pay for everything with cash, check, or debit card at the time of purchase. But, before performing plastic surgery all of your surplus dollars should be directed toward building a small emergency fund to handle any unplanned expenses. A good start would be a minimum of $1,000 to $1,500 depending on your income and ability to raise cash. It may be necessary to look

> *Owe no man anything, but to love one another: for he that loveth another hath fulfilled the law*—**Romans 13:8**

at some of your personal belongings and consider a garage sale to establish a reserve fund. If for some reason you have to use some of your reserves, you must replenish them immediately.

Now that you have established your reserve fund, you must continue to pray and ask for God's guidance. Remember that staying faithful will provide you the needed comfort during these troubling times. Learn to trust God and rely on His provision rather than on credit and borrowing. Throughout this process extreme discipline must be maintained concerning spending and we must learn to be content with what we have, realizing that debt freedom will be worth all of the sacrifices and all of the discipline.

The next step would be to sit down and make a list of all of your creditors. You will need to list everyone that you owe. List the name & address of every creditor and their balances, interest rates, and minimum payments. From this you are in the first phase to becoming financially free. Now that we have a list of creditor(s) available we need to decide who gets what. By now you should have developed a budget. In that budget you have identified and determined what needs to be cut to create a surplus. It is from the surplus that will allow you to get out of debt. Whatever surplus you come up with will now be considered your **ACCELERATOR.** Your new accelerator will help you get out of debt faster.

Now that you have a list of your creditors, and have created a surplus by decreasing your lifestyle, it is time to go to work. On a separate sheet of paper write the names of your creditors. In a column next to their names list the total amount owed. In a second column list the minimum monthly payment. The next step requires you to clear your mind of everything you have ever heard about paying off debt. It is time to do something different.

It has been said, *"The definition of insanity is doing the same thing over and over again, and expecting a different result"*. If you have been going through life with the same habits, how can you expect something different to happen unless you change? Next, take the total amount you owe and divide that amount by the minimum payment. This in of itself means nothing, but what this number represents is rough fully how many months it is going to take to pay this particular debt off just by making the minimum payments.

Example: If you had a $700 balance on a credit card and the minimum payment is $50. If you divide 700 by 50 you will get an answer of 14.

This number says that you have approximately 14 months to pay this balance by making just the minimum payments—In reality, if you factor in the average interest rate of 14% it would take you 16 months to pay the balance. This number is known as the *payoff priority.* You would repeat this process for all your creditors. Now that you have determined the payoff priority for each creditor, these numbers indicate which debt you should pay off first. The creditor with the lowest number would be the first debt to be paid off. What this process really reveals is that if all else remains the same and you continued to make minimum payments the creditor with the lowest payoff priority would be the first debt to be paid off. Interest rate is not the issue at this point; our goal here is to accelerate the date in which this debt will be paid by using our surplus. Even if your surplus were nominal, by adding only $100 extra dollars to each minimum payment, it would take several months off the time to pay the balance.

In the example below, *Figure 1* illustrates the debt payoff priority of a typical family with various types of debts.

Name of debt	Total Balance	Minimum Payment	Divisor	Pay-off Priority	Margin Roll-Up	Pay-Off Months
1	2	3	4	5	6	7
Discover	$3,264	$66	49.5	4	$401	8.1
Sears	$4,008	$88	45.5	3	$335	12.0
AT&T	$2,797	$62	45.3	2	$247	11.3
MBNA	$3,227	$185	17.4	1	$185	17.4
TOTAL	$13,296	$401				
Accelerator				0		
Total monthy payment				$401		

Figure 1

In our example, this couple has $13,296 in consumer debt, making only the minimum payments it would take three years and seven months to pay off all their debt. By using the priority payoff, method and adding an accelerator of $300 this same family would be debt free

in one year and ten months. That is one year and nine months earlier.
In addition, they would save $1,735.66 in interest.

Once you realize what a powerful mathematical tool this is,
finding additional money for your accelerator will not be a problem.
Imagine debt that would normally take a life to pay back gone in just
a few months. Remember, the month after a debt is eliminated; you
take that minimum payment plus your accelerator and add it to the
next debt. This process may go against everything that you may have
been taught about money but it works. By the time, you get to other
larger payments like a vehicle or even your mortgage your accelerator
will be quit large. Assuming you follow this payoff priority method,
you will soon find yourself in the position to say *"good-bye"* to credit
forever.

Debt-free living is still God's plan for His people today. Once
families have realized debt freedom, a radical change in lifestyle and
a reevaluation of family values should be considered to help prevent
similar debt situations from reoccurring. The blessings of becoming
debt free go far beyond the financial area. They extend to the spiritual
and marital realms as well. No one who is financially bound can be
spiritually free. In addition, the effects of financial bondage on a
marriage relationship are measurable in the statistics of failed
marriages. Approximately 50 percent of all first marriages fail, and
finances are listed as the leading cause of divorce by a factor of four
to one. Therefore, it is advisable for God's people to make debt
freedom a top priority in their families.

God expects his people to be the head and not the tail.   In
Deuteronomy 28:12-14, God says that if Christians follow his word
other nations will follow us. His people will lend and not borrow, this
has been promised to us if we keep his commandments.

*"And the Lord will make you the head and not the tail; you shall be
above only, and not beneath, if you heed the commandments of the
Lord you God, which I command you today, and are careful to
observe them."* —Deuteronomy 28:13

5. <u>Give</u>

As we become better stewards we will be given a tremendous new responsibility. When we gain control of our financial lives we now have the opportunity to become an asset to the kingdom of God. In step two, giving of the tithe is only the beginning. The work of God speaks about sacrificial giving, *"But this I say: He who sows sparingly will also reap sparingly, and he who sows bountifully will also reap bountifully. So let each one give as he purposes in his heart not grudgingly or of necessity; for God loves a cheerful giver. And God is able to make all grace abound toward you, that you always having all sufficiency in all things, may have an abundance for every good work"* **II Corinthians 9:6-8**, this type of giving is done out of surplus. God's system is simple, the more you give the more you will have to give.

First every Christian can and should tithe regularly. This is done out of love for God, and because he asked us to give a tenth of our increase. Once you have gained control of your finances you should have a surplus. This money would be the money above and beyond your family's basic needs. When God blesses you with abundance, you are now obligated to seek his guidance on how to help others. One of the greatest joys in life is the ability to help someone else in need. This is what God wants and when we give we should do so with a sense of anticipating the Lord to provide a material increase. Giving allows God to remain priority in our lives, because we must continue to rely on His provisions for the future.

The Problem Revisited

Seldom do we realize we are in debt until it is too late. In many cases, debt is like rust; by the time, you see a sign of rust the damage is already done. The North American economic system has fooled you to think only in terms of monthly payments. If you find yourself asking how much are the payments that is a good sign that you cannot afford it. When we purchase that big-ticket item and agree to make monthly payments, seldom do we think about how much this item is really costing us.

Consumers have been programmed to think that you need credit; we are constantly told keep "good credit" Why? So we can get more credit. Whenever someone offers you credit he or she are not giving you anything If you are offered a MASTERcard with a balance of $5,000, are you really getting $5,000? NO! In fact, you are simply moving up the date which you can make purchases with money that you have not earned — at a cost no doubt. By taking credit you are not adding a single cent to your wealth

The sad reality is that as long as you are in the monthly payment frame of mind then you are literally giving away your future. Giving away future retirement, future wealth that could be used for a more useful purpose, a heavenly purpose. In addition, this is being done just for a few things today, the true cost of debt is more than we realize. Then you wake up one day only to realize that you cannot stop working you have too much debt.

Credit Card Math

There are 7,000 institutions issuing credit cards (Visa, MasterCard) in the United States, 30,000 different credit card programs (Visa, MasterCard, Discover, American Express and Diners Club), 200 million new credit cards issued in 2000 with an average

24

charge per transaction (Visa, MasterCard) of approximately $70.00. Source: CardWeb.com, Inc. The average interest rate charged on credit cards is approximately 14% with the highest credit card interest rate being charged by CompuCredit at 41%. In 2001, the average U.S. household with at least one credit card owed $8,562, up from $2,985 in 1990. The average credit card holder has 6.5 credit cards while the average number of cards per household is 14.3. Source: CardWeb.com, Inc.

The top three source of revenue for credit card companies is 1) Interest 2) Merchant fees and 3) Late fees. In June 1996, the U.S. Supreme Court ruled that commercial banks could charge whatever fees they want on credit cards, anywhere in the country. The 1996 ruling preempts state laws regarding card fees for an out-of-state issuer. Since then, late fee revenue generated to bank credit card issuers has soared from $1.7 billion to $7.3 billion, annually. Since 1996, average late fees have more than doubled, from an average of $13.28 to $29.84. Survey found that 58.3% of consumers say they have been hit with late fees during the past year (2001). Source: CardWeb.com, Inc. As credit card companies start aggressive marketing campaigns, consumers are being flooded with crafty offers. The average household receives eight card offers per month.

Less equals more

At first thought the simple notion of the lower the interest rate charged the less you pay. That thought would be true under normal circumstances; unfortunately, when we are dealing with credit card companies' things are not equal. While consumers are continuing to struggle, credit card companies' profits have more than double. According to cardweb.com, between 1995 and 1999 credit card companies' profits rose from $7.3 billion to $20 billion. The card industry has and will continue to keep consumers in debt with crafty credit card math.

When you think about it, if you have a balance of $5,000 on a credit card and the minimum payment is $150 per month, it might be very tempting to transfer the balance to another that only requires a $100 minimum balance. This type of transaction happens all the time, and that is exactly what the credit card companies want you to do.

The required minimum payment on a credit card is normally calculated as a percentage of the outstanding balance. Therefore, as your balance goes down then your minimum payment goes down. When we continue to pay the minimum payment every month then we are merely extending the length of the loan, and increasing the amount of interest paid. Minimum payments usually range from 2% to 3% of the outstanding balance. The lower the percentage the lower your minimum payment, which means you, stay in debt longer and pay more interest. In our previous example, a $5,000 balance with a 3% minimum payment of $150 with a 17% interest rate, it would cost you $4,296 in interest and take 18 years to pay off. On the other had if you transfer the balance to a card that has a 2% minimum payment your payment would drop to $100 per month, and it would cost you $11,304 in interest and take you 40 years to pay back.

The following table shows that just because you are transferring to a lower interest rate card, it could end up costing you more in the long run

Table 1

Card	Min. % Pmt	First Month's Pmt	Interest Cost	Payoff
A	1.67%	$83.50	$25,354.00	81 yrs
B	2.00%	100.00	11,304.00	40 yrs
C	2.50%	125.00	6,210.00	24 yrs
D	3.00%	150.00	4,296.00	18 yrs

What a Difference a Fraction of a Percent Makes

Based on a $5,000 credit card balance a 17% interest rate.

What table one tells you is that there is not a trick to getting out of debt. Who would have thought that a 19.8% credit card could take you about half as long to pay back as a 13.5% card? The bottom line is, when it comes to credit cards or any loan the more you pay the less you pay in the end.

More than anything else debt robs more people of their freedom. Borrowing from the world puts a barrier between God and us. The ease of getting credit makes it very difficult for Christians to trust that God will supply our needs. Instead of pray for guidance, we borrow the money to get the things we want. The bible does not say that it is wrong to borrow money, Proverbs 22:7 warns about the relation of the borrower and the lender. The bible goes further to talk about serving two masters. It is possible for Christian and everyone else for that matter to live without debt – even today. During difficult times, it is important for us to lean not onto our own understanding, but instead trust God to do what is right in our lives. As we learn to put more trust in God, he will reveal more of himself in our lives. *"Trust in the Lord with all your heart and lean not on your own understanding; In all your ways acknowledge Him and He shall direct your paths"* – Proverbs 3:5-6

Consolidation the Truth

When it comes to loan consolidation, this strategy rarely works. Consumers fall for the good feeling they get when they consolidate their loans. However, consolidation does nothing more than transfer several little loans to one big loan. If the true problem — which in most cases is spending more than you make is never addressed; then you are doomed to repeat those mistakes and make an already bad situation worse. Often times when Christians seek relief in the form of a debt consolidation loan they find themselves in more debt. This is because of the lack of planning. *"For which of you, intending to build a tower does not sit down first and count the cost, whether he has enough to finish it"* – **Luke 14:28**

Consolidation is not just a matter of trying to lower your interest rate. It is not the interest that is the problem. It's the behavior that causes the credit crunch. Truth be told, once you are in debt it is a little late to be concerned about interest, that should have been a thought before the purchase. Debt consolidation is about creating a plan, taking control of your finances, and making wise decision. Mathematically consolidation makes sense, but only after you have prayed and asked God for guidance and vowed not to use debt (credit card, loans, etc) as a means to get things that you do not necessarily need. The first step in deciding whether or not to consolidate is to take time to figure out how much you owe. Once you have done this and prayed for guidance, then make the choice to get the best consolidation possible. However, if you don't change your habits, you could end up forking over even more money than if you had just paid your bills at the higher interest rate. After prayer and thought you may decide that you would be better off just to keep paying on the loans that you currently have.

CASE STUDY

Michael & Cassandra Boyd are your typical middle-income family. Michael a 32-year-old auto mechanic and Sandra 29 year old nurse have been married nine years and have one-child Kevin 7 years old. Both Michael and Cassandra work outside the home, their combined gross monthly income is $4,896 per month. The Boyd's are currently renting and desperately want to purchase a home but just cannot seem to start saving money.

The Boyd's are currently $33,400 dollars in debt that consist of $18,500 in vehicle debt, $5,200 in student loan debt, and $9,200 in consumer debt (Credit Card Debt). Like 70% of Americans, the Boyd's are living from paycheck to paycheck. The Boyd's do not currently operate from a household budget

Take a moment to review the Boyd's situation and the results achieved from Alliance Financial Ministries, Inc.

Lonnie R. Mathews

MONTHLY INCOME AND EXPENSES

Gross Income from all sources			Medical Expenses		
			Doctor visits	30.00	
Salary	4,896.00		Dentist visits		
Social Security			Drugs		
VA Benefits			Other		
Other Income			**TOTAL MEDICAL**		$ 30.00
TOTAL INCOME		$ 4,896.00			
			Miscellaneous		
MINUS:			Toiletries	25.00	
			Beauty, Barber	115.00	
Tithes		$ 50.00	Dry Cleaning	53.00	
Taxes (Fed., State, FICA)		$ 1,548.00	Lunches	95.00	
			Gifts		
MAXIMUM SPENDABLE INCOME		$ 3,298.00	Other		
			TOTAL MISC		$ 288.00
Housing					
Mortgage	725.00		**Child Care**		
Electricity	129.00		Day care/Tution	66.00	
Gas			Transportation		
Water			Materials		
Sanitation			**TOTAL CHILD CARE**		$ 66.00
Telephone	75.00				
Maintenance	50.00		**Savings / Investments**		
Other	50.00		Savings		
TOTAL HOUSING		$ 1,029.00	Investments 401(k)		
			TOTAL SAVINGS		
FOOD	100.00	$ 100.00	**Enter./Rec.**		
			Eating Out	150.00	
Automobile(s)			Baby Sitters	25.00	
Payments	776.00		Activities	60.00	
Gas & Oil	312.00		Vaction		
Insurance	118.00		Other	30.00	
License/Taxes			**TOTAL ENT./REC.**		$ 265.00
Maint./Repairs					
TOTAL AUTOMOBILE(S)		$ 1,206.00			
			TOTAL EXPENSES:		$ 3,332.00
Insurance					
Life *(outside work)*	70.00		INCOME VERSUS EXPENSES		
Other			Max Spendable Income		$ 3,298.00
TOTAL INSURANCE		$ 70.00	Less Expenses		$ 3,332.00
			SURPLUS INCOME		$ (34.00)
Debts					
Credit Card	145.00				
Loans	78.00				
Other Debt	55.00				
TOTAL DEBTS		$ 278.00			

Lonnie R. Mathews

FINANCIAL STATEMENT

ASSETS *(what I own)*

Liquid Assets [1]

Checking Acct	$	55.00
Savings Acct	$	125.00
Money Mkt		
CD's		
Total Liquid Assets	**$**	**180.00**

Invested Assets [2]

IRA		
Cash Value Ins	$	2,500.00
Mutual Funds		
Stocks		
401(k)		
Total Invested	**$**	**2,500.00**

Other Assets [3]

Household items	$	5,000.00
Nissan	$	3,000.00
Toyota	$	12,000.00
Personal Items	$	8,000.00
Total Other Assets	**$ 28,000.00**

TOTAL ASSSETS   **$ 30,680.00**

LIABILITIES *(What I owe)*

Toyota	$	16,000.00
Visa	$	6,800.00
Student Loan	$	5,200.00
Nissan	$	2,500.00
Wachovia	$	1,800.00
Sears	$	800.00
Best Financial	$	300.00

TOTAL LIABILITIES **$ 33,400.00**

NET WORTH   **$ (2,720.00)**

(Assets - Liabilities)

Lonnie R. Mathews

List of Debts

To whom Owed	Balance	Min. Payment	Interest Rate	Months Behind	% of total Debt
Company Toyota Motor Co. Address PO Box 34958 City Wilmington State DE Zip 75900 Acct. # 1299-5978-12-4456 Telephone #	$16,000.00	$480.00	8.0%	0	48.0%
Company MBNA Address PO Box 40499 City Anytown State MD Zip 89776 Acct. # 3980-0987 Telephone #	$6,800.00	$120.00	16.9%	0	20.0%
Company Federal Student Loans Address 349 Anyway Dr. City Smallville State NE Zip 98765 Acct. # 88956 Telephone #	$5,200.00	$55.00	5.5%	0	16.0%
Company National Bank Address 9483 Main St City Bigville State AL Zip 35449 Acct. # 788E44955A Telephone #	$2,500.00	$296.00	7.5%	0	7.0%
Company Wachovia Bank Address 191 Peachtree City Atlanta State GA Zip 35948 Acct. # 45-9987 Telephone #	$1,800.00	$50.00	6.8%	0	5.0%
Company Sears Credit Address PO Box 87632 City Houston State TX Zip 77564 Acct. # 013-8878-3659-50 Telephone #	$800.00	$25.00	21.0%	0	2.0%
Company Best Financial Address 8388 South St. City Houston State TX Zip 77596 Acct. # 2-98723 Telephone #	$300.00	$28.00	29.0%	0	1.0%

Lonnie R. Mathews

MONTHLY INCOME AND EXPENSES

Gross Income from all sources

Salary	4,896.00
Social Security	
VA Benefits	
Other Income	

TOTAL INCOME $ 4,896.00

MINUS:

Tithes	$	489.60
Taxes (Fed., State, FICA)	$	1,548.00

MAXIMUM SPENDABLE INCOME $ 2,858.40

Housing

Mortgage	725.00		
Electricity	129.00		
Gas			
Water			
Sanitation			
Telephone	32.00		
Maintenance	29.00		
Other	31.00		
TOTAL HOUSING		$	946.00

FOOD   100.00 $ 100.00

Automobile(s)

Payments	480.00		
Gas & Oil	312.00		
Insurance	80.00		
License/Taxes			
Maint./Repairs			
TOTAL AUTOMOBILE(S)		$	872.00

Insurance

Life *(outside work)*	23.00		
Other			
TOTAL INSURANCE		$	23.00

Debts

Credit Card	145.00		
Loans	78.00		
Other Debt	55.00		
TOTAL DEBTS		$	278.00

Medical Expenses

Doctor visits	30.00		
Dentist visits			
Drugs			
Other			
TOTAL MEDICAL		$	30.00

Miscellaneous

Toiletries	25.00		
Beauty, Barber	70.00		
Dry Cleaning	20.00		
Lunches	25.00		
Gifts			
Other			
TOTAL MISC		$	140.00

Child Care

Day care/Tution	66.00		
Transportation			
Materials			
TOTAL CHILD CARE		$	66.00

Savings / Investments

Savings	50.00		
Investments 401(k)			
TOTAL SAVINGS		$	50.00

Enter./Rec.

Eating Out	53.00		
Baby Sitters	15.00		
Activities	30.00		
Vaction			
Other	30.00		
TOTAL ENT./REC.		$	128.00

TOTAL EXPENSES: $ 2,633.00

INCOME VERSUS EXPENSES

Max Spendable Income	$	2,858.40
Less Expenses	$	2,633.00
SURPLUS INCOME	$	225.40

Lonnie R. Mathews

FINANCIAL STATEMENT

ASSETS *(what I own)*

Liquid Assets ₁

Checking Acct	$	100.00
Savings Acct	$	750.00
Money Mkt		
CD's		
Total Liquid Assets	**$**	**850.00**

Invested Assets ₂

IRA	
Cash Value Ins	
Mutual Funds	
Stocks	
401(k)	
Total Invested	**$ -**

Other Assets ₃

Household items	$	4,600.00
Nissan	$	3,000.00
Toyota	$	12,000.00
Personal Items	$	7,750.00
Total Other Assets	**$ 27,350.00**	

TOTAL ASSSETS   **$ 28,200.00**

LIABILITIES *(What I owe)*

Toyota	$	16,000.00
Visa	$	6,800.00
Student Loan	$	5,200.00
Line of credit	$	1,800.00
Sears	$	800.00
Best Finance	$	300.00

TOTAL LIABILITIE$ $ 30,900.00

NET WORTH   **$ (2,700.00)**

(Assets - Liabilities)

Lonnie R. Mathews

Alliance Financial Ministries, Inc.

A Non-profit Christian Debt Management Company

10101 Southwest Freeway Ste. 400 Houston, Texas 77074 Tel. 1.888.385.1521

Debt Pay-off Priority

Name of debt	Total Balance	Minimum Payment	Divisor	Pay-off Priority	Margin Roll-Up	Pay-Off Months
1	2	3	4	5	6	7
Federal Student Loan	$5,200	$55	94.5	7	$984	5.3
Toyota Motor Co.	$16,000	$185	86.4	6	$929	17.2
MBNA	$6,800	$120	56.7	5	$744	9.1
Wachovia	$1,800	$50	36.0	4	$624	2.9
Sears	$800	$25	32.0	3	$574	1.4
Best Financial	$300	$28	10.7	2	$549	0.5
National Bank	$2,500	$296	8.4	1	$521	4.8

TOTAL   **$33,400**   **$759**

My Accelerator Margin $225

Total monthy payment $984

Lonnie R. Mathews

Percentage Guide

Annual Income			$ 58,752.00		

Gross Income Per Month $ 4,896.00

    Tithes $ 489.00 *(10% of gross)*
    Taxes $ 1,548.00

Maximun Spendable Income (MS $ 2,859.00

	%	X	MSI	=	$Amount$
Housing	30%	X	$ 2,859.00	=	$857.70
Food	11%	X	$ 2,859.00	=	$314.49
Automobile	13%	X	$ 2,859.00	=	$371.67
Insurance	5%	X	$ 2,859.00	=	$142.95
Debts	5%	X	$ 2,859.00	=	$142.95
Ent / Rec	7%	X	$ 2,859.00	=	$200.13
Clothing	7%	X	$ 2,859.00	=	$200.13
Savings	5%	X	$ 2,859.00	=	$142.95
Medical	4%	X	$ 2,859.00	=	$114.36
Miscellaneous	5%	X	$ 2,859.00	=	$142.95
Savings / Inv.1	8%	X	$ 2,859.00	=	$228.72
Childcare / School	**5%**	**X**	**$2,859.00**	**=**	**$0.00**
TOTAL	100%		N/A		$2,859.00

1 If you have this expense, this precentage must be deducted from other budget categories

Lonnie R. Mathews

Case Study revisited

After careful examination the Boyd's situation is no different than the average American family. They are victims of overspending and not saying no to the person in the mirror. During their first counseling session, the Boyd's filled out a monthly income and expense. This will give an accurate picture of where the Boyd's money is going, and the following is the result:

- According to the percentage guide Michael and Sandra are spending too much on housing expenses.
- The Boyd's are also spending way to much on automobiles
- Two other categories that are holding Michael and Sandra back are entertainment and miscellaneous expenses.

An Alliance Financial counselor made the following recommendations to help the Boyd's on the road to recovery. The counselor noticed that there was little to no savings, so when an unscheduled event happens they are forced to use debt.

1. The Boyd's should consider having a garage sale and use the funds to establish an emergency fund
2. Next the Boyd's should cash in the cash value insurance policy and use the proceeds to pay off the loan on the Nissan. Because there is a need for insurance, term insurance should be purchased.
3. The Miscellaneous and Entertainment categories must be examined carefully and cut drastically.

After considering the counselor's advice the Boyd's were able to get a handle on their finances. By selling personal items around the house the Boyd's now have an emergency fund of $850. This should only be used to take care of any unforeseen expense that may come up.

By downgrading their current telephone service and getting rid of the extra line, as well as finding a less expensive Internet service provider the Boyd's were able to get their housing expense in line according to the spending guide. Next by cashing in the whole life policy with a cash value of $2,500 and using the proceeds to pay off the balance on the Nissan automobile the Boyd's were able to free up an additional $296 per month.

Because there is a need for insurance the Boyd's decided to purchase a twenty-year term policy that not only gave them more coverage but also reduced their cost from $70 per month to only $23 per month. The Boyd's had to take a careful look at the last two categories. The counselor determined that the Boyd's were spending too much money eating out, as well as other items like dry cleaning beauty treatments and activities. If the Boyd's could some how practice self-denial they could now have a surplus of $225 per month for debt reduction. Plus more importantly the Boyd's are now tithing $489 per month 10% of their income.

With their newfound freedom the counselor has instructed the Boyd's to use the surplus income to reduce debt. Given their current situation, by making only the minimum payments it would take the Boyd's 4 years and 7 months to pay of their existing debt. However, by rolling the surplus of $225 dollar into debt reduction the Boyd's would be debt free in 3 years. Once all debts have been paid, the Boyd's can begin building wealth. Now by taking the money they were paying debt with, in 3 years the Boyd's will have saved almost $37,000.

FORMS

Lonnie R. Mathews

MONTHLY INCOME AND EXPENSES

Gross Income from all sources

Salary _____
Social Security _____
VA Benefits _____
Other Income _____

TOTAL INCOME _____

MINUS:

Tithes _____
Taxes (Fed., State, FICA) _____

MAXIMUM SPENDABLE INCOME _____

Housing
Mortgage _____
Electricity _____
Gas _____
Water _____
Sanitation _____
Telephone _____
Maintenance _____
Other _____
TOTAL HOUSING _____

FOOD _____

Automobile(s)
Payments _____
Gas & Oil _____
Insurance _____
License/Taxes _____
Maint./Repairs _____
TOTAL AUTOMOBILE(S) _____

Insurance
Life *(outside work)* _____
Other _____
TOTAL INSURANCE _____

Debts
Credit Card _____
Loans _____
Other Debt _____

Medical Expenses
Doctor visits _____
Dentist visits _____
Drugs _____
Other _____
TOTAL MEDICAL _____

Miscellaneous
Toiletries _____
Beauty, Barber _____
Dry Cleaning _____
Lunches _____
Gifts _____
Other _____
TOTAL MISC _____

Child Care
Day care/Tution _____
Transportation _____
Materials _____
TOTAL CHILD CARE _____

Savings / Investments
Savings _____
Investments 401(k) _____
TOTAL SAVINGS _____

Enter./Rec.
Eating Out _____
Baby Sitters _____
Activities _____
Vaction _____
Other _____
TOTAL ENT./REC. _____

TOTAL EXPENSES: _____

INCOME VERSUS EXPENSES
Max Spendable Income
Less Expenses
SURPLUS INCOME _____

Lonnie R. Mathews

FINANCIAL STATEMENT

ASSETS *(what I own)*   **LIABILITIES** *(What I owe)*

Liquid Assets[1]

Checking Acct	_____	Mortgage	_____
Savings Acct	_____	Auto Loan 1	_____
Money Mkt	_____	Auto Loan 2	_____
CD's	_____	Credit Cards	_____
_____	_____	Other Loans	_____

Total Liquid Assets _____

Invested Assets[2]

IRA	_____
Cash Value Ins	_____
Mutual Funds	_____
Stocks	_____
401(k)	_____
_____	_____

Total Invested _____

TOTAL LIABILITIES _____

Other Assets[3]

NET WORTH _____

Household items	_____
Nissan	_____
Toyota	_____
Personal Items	_____
_____	_____
_____	_____
_____	_____

(Assets - Liabilities)

Total Other Assets _____

TOTAL ASSSETS _____

Lonnie R. Mathews

List of Debts

To whom Owed	Balance	Min. Payment	Interest Rate	Months Behind	% of total Debt
Company_____ Address_____ City_____ State_____ Zip_____ Acct. #_____ Telephone #_____					
Company_____ Address_____ City_____ State_____ Zip_____ Acct. #_____ Telephone #_____					
Company_____ Address_____ City_____ State_____ Zip_____ Acct. #_____ Telephone #_____					
Company_____ Address_____ City_____ State_____ Zip_____ Acct. #_____ Telephone #_____					
Company_____ Address_____ City_____ State_____ Zip_____ Acct. #_____ Telephone #_____					

feel free to make as many copies as need!

Lonnie R. Mathews

Percentage Guide

Annual Income _____

Gross Income Per Month $ _____ -

    Tithes _____ *(10% of gross)*
    Taxes _____

Maximun Spendable Income *(MS* $ _____ -

	%	X	MSI	=	$Amount$
Housing	30%	X	$ -	=	_____
Food	11%	X	$ -	=	_____
Automobile	13%	X	$ -	=	_____
Insurance	5%	X	$ -	=	_____
Debts	5%	X	$ -	=	_____
Ent / Rec	7%	X	$ -	=	_____
Clothing	7%	X	$ -	=	_____
Savings	5%	X	$ -	=	_____
Medical	4%	X	$ -	=	_____
Miscellaneous	5%	X	$ -	=	_____
Savings / Inv.1	8%	X	$ -	=	_____
Childcare / School	**5%**	**X**	$0.00	=	_____
TOTAL	100%		N/A		_____

1 If you have this expense, this precentage must be deducted from other budget categories

Lonnie R. Mathews

Payday Spending Plan

Annual Income $_____

Gross Monthly Income $_____

Monthly Payment	Description	Payday / /	Payday / /	Actually Spent	Difference+ OR -
Maximum Spendable Income **(Your bring home pay)**		$	$	$	$
Tithes *(gross income x 10%)*					
Housing *(Mortgage; Rent)*					
Utlities *(Cable,Electric, Gas, Water, Maint.)*					
Automobile *(Pmt., Fuel, Maint.)*					
Insurance *(Auto,Life, Disa, Etc.)*					
Savings *(Uexpected Expenses)*					
Debts *(Credit Cards, Loans)*					
Food *(Groceries)*					
Recreation *(Eat-out, Lunch, Movies, Etc)*					
Miscellanous *(Personal Care, Haircut)*					
Child Care *(Daycare, Diapers, Etc.)*					
Other *(other expenses)*					
Other *(other expenses)*					
Other *(other expenses)*					
Other *(other expenses)*					
Other *(other expenses)*					
$$$ BLOW $$$ *(spend uselessly)*					
Total Income		$	$		
Total Spent		$	$		$
Balance		**$0**	**$0**		

Make enough copies to complete two months of paydays

Lonnie R. Mathews

Alliance Financial Ministries, Inc.

A Non-profit Christian Debt Management Company

10101 Southwest Freeway Ste. 400 ?Houston, Texas 77074?Tel. 1.888.385.1521

Debt Pay-off Priority

Name of debt 1	Total Balance 2	Minimum Payment 3	Divisor 4	Pay-off Priority 5	Margin Roll-Up 6	Pay-Off Months 7

TOTAL

My Accelerator Margin

Total monthy payment

Lonnie R. Mathews

APPENDIX A

Lonnie R. Mathews

THE FAIR DEBT COLLECTION PRACTICES ACT

As amended by Public Law 104-208, 110 Stat. 3009 (Sept. 30, 1996)

To amend the Consumer Credit Protection Act to prohibit abusive practices by debt collectors.

Be it enacted by the Senate and House of Representatives of the United States of America in Congress assembled, That the Consumer Credit Protection Act (15 U.S.C. 1601 et seq.) is amended by adding at the end thereof the following new title:

TITLE VIII - DEBT COLLECTION PRACTICES [Fair Debt Collection Practices Act]

Sec.

§ 801. Short Title [15 USC 1601 note]

This title may be cited as the "Fair Debt Collection Practices Act."

§ 802. Congressional findings and declarations of purpose [15 USC 1692]

(a) There is abundant evidence of the use of abusive, deceptive, and unfair debt collection practices by many debt collectors. Abusive debt collection practices contribute to the number of personal bankruptcies, to marital instability, to the loss of jobs, and to invasions of individual privacy.

(b) Existing laws and procedures for redressing these injuries are inadequate to protect consumers.

(c) Means other than misrepresentation or other abusive debt collection practices are available for the effective collection of debts.

(d) Abusive debt collection practices are carried on to a substantial extent in interstate commerce and through means and instrumentalities of such commerce. Even where abusive debt collection practices are purely intrastate in character, they nevertheless directly affect interstate commerce.

(e) It is the purpose of this title to eliminate abusive debt collection practices by debt collectors, to insure that those debt collectors who refrain from using abusive debt collection practices are not competitively disadvantaged, and to promote consistent State action to protect consumers against debt collection abuses.

§ 803. Definitions [15 USC 1692a]

As used in this title —

(1) The term "Commission" means the Federal Trade Commission.

(2) The term "communication" means the conveying of information regarding a debt directly or indirectly to any person through any medium.

(3) The term "consumer" means any natural person obligated or allegedly obligated to pay any debt.

(4) The term "creditor" means any person who offers or extends credit creating a debt or to whom a debt is owed, but such term does not include any person to the extent that he receives an assignment or transfer of a debt in default solely for the purpose of facilitating collection of such debt for another.

(5) The term "debt" means any obligation or alleged obligation of a consumer to pay money arising out of a transaction in which the money, property, insurance or services which are the subject of the transaction are primarily for personal, family, or household purposes, whether or not such obligation has been reduced to judgment.

(6) The term "debt collector" means any person who uses any instrumentality of interstate commerce or the mails in any business the principal purpose of which is the collection of any debts, or who regularly collects or attempts to collect, directly or indirectly, debts owed or due or asserted to be owed or due another. Notwithstanding the exclusion provided by clause (F) of the last sentence of this paragraph, the term includes any creditor who, in the process of collecting his own debts, uses any name other than his own which would indicate that a third person is collecting or attempting to collect such debts. For the purpose of section 808(6), such term also includes any person who uses any instrumentality of interstate commerce or the mails in any business the principal purpose of which is the enforcement of security interests. The term does not include –

(A) Any officer or employee of a creditor while, in the name of the creditor, collecting debts for such creditor;

(B) Any person while acting as a debt collector for another person, both of whom are related by common ownership or affiliated by corporate control, if the person acting as a debt collector does so only for persons to whom it is so related or affiliated and if the principal business of such person is not the collection of debts;

(C) Any officer or employee of the United States or any State to the extent that collecting or attempting to collect any debt is in the performance of his official duties;

(D) Any person while serving or attempting to serve legal process on any other person in connection with the judicial enforcement of any debt;

(E) Any nonprofit organization which, at the request of consumers, performs bona fide consumer credit counseling and assists consumers in the liquidation of their debts by receiving payments from such consumers and distributing such amounts to creditors; and

(F) any person collecting or attempting to collect any debt owed or due or asserted to be owed or due another to the extent such activity (i) is incidental to a bona fide fiduciary obligation or a bona fide escrow arrangement; (ii) concerns a debt which was originated by such person; (iii) concerns a debt which was not in default at the time it was obtained by such person; or (iv) concerns a debt obtained by such person as a secured party in a commercial credit transaction involving the creditor.

(7) The term "location information" means a consumer's place of abode and his telephone number at such place, or his place of employment.

(8) The term "State" means any State, territory, or possession of the United States, the District of Columbia, the Commonwealth of Puerto Rico, or any political subdivision of any of the foregoing.

§ 804. Acquisition of location information [15 USC 1692b]

Any debt collector communicating with any person other than the consumer for the purpose of acquiring location information about the consumer shall —

(1) Identify him, state that he is confirming or correcting location information concerning the consumer, and, only if expressly requested, identify his employer;

(2) Not state that such consumer owes any debt;

(3) Not communicate with any such person more than once unless requested to do so by such person or unless the debt collector reasonably believes that the earlier response of such person is erroneous or incomplete and that such person now has correct or complete location information;

(4) Not communicate by post card;

(5) Not use any language or symbol on any envelope or in the contents of any communication effected by the mails or telegram that indicates that the debt collector is in the debt collection business or that the communication relates to the collection of a debt; and

(6) After the debt collector knows the consumer is represented by an attorney with regard to the subject debt and has knowledge of, or can readily ascertain, such attorney's name and address, not communicate with any person other than that attorney, unless the attorney fails to respond within a reasonable period of time to the communication from the debt collector.

§ 805. Communication in connection with debt collection [15 USC 1692c]

(a) COMMUNICATION WITH THE CONSUMER GENERALLY. Without the prior consent of the consumer given directly to the debt collector or the express permission of a court of competent jurisdiction, a debt collector may not communicate with a consumer in connection with the collection of any debt —

(1) at any unusual time or place or a time or place known or which should be known to be inconvenient to the consumer. In the absence of knowledge of circumstances to the contrary, a debt collector shall assume that the convenient time for communicating with a consumer is after 8 o'clock antemeridian and before 9 o'clock postmeridian, local time at the consumer's location;

(2) if the debt collector knows the consumer is represented by an attorney with respect to such debt and has knowledge of, or can readily ascertain, such attorney's name and address, unless the attorney fails to respond within a reasonable period of time to a communication from the debt collector or unless the attorney consents to direct communication with the consumer; or

(3) At the consumer's place of employment if the debt collector knows or has reason to know that the consumer's employer prohibits the consumer from receiving such communication.

(b) COMMUNICATION WITH THIRD PARTIES. Except as provided in section 804, without the prior consent of the consumer given directly to the debt collector, or the express permission of a court of competent jurisdiction, or as reasonably necessary to effectuate a post judgment judicial remedy, a debt collector may not communicate, in connection with the collection of any debt, with any person other than a consumer, his attorney, a consumer reporting agency if otherwise permitted by law, the creditor, the attorney of the creditor, or the attorney of the debt collector.

(c) CEASING COMMUNICATION. If a consumer notifies a debt collector in writing that the consumer refuses to pay a debt or that the consumer wishes the debt collector to cease further communication with the consumer, the debt collector shall not communicate further with the consumer with respect to such debt, except —

(1) To advise the consumer that the debt collector's further efforts are being terminated:

(2) To notify the consumer that the debt collector or creditor may invoke specified remedies which are ordinarily invoked by such debt collector or creditor; or

(3) Where applicable, to notify the consumer that the debt collector or creditor intends to invoke a specified remedy.

If such notice from the consumer is made by mail, notification shall be complete upon receipt.

(d) For the purpose of this section, the term "consumer" includes the consumer's spouse, parent (if the consumer is a minor), guardian, executor, or administrator.

§ 806. Harassment or abuse [15 USC 1692d]

A debt collector may not engage in any conduct the natural consequence of which is to harass, oppress, or abuse any person in connection with the collection of a debt. Without limiting the general application of the foregoing, the following conduct is a violation of this section:

(1) The use or threat of use of violence or other criminal means to harm the physical person, reputation, or property of any person.

(2) The use of obscene or profane language or language the natural consequence of which is to abuse the hearer or reader.

(3) The publication of a list of consumers who allegedly refuse to pay debts, except to a consumer reporting agency or to persons meeting the requirements of section 603(f) or 604(3)[1] of this Act.

(4) The advertisement for sale of any debt to coerce payment of the debt.

(5) Causing a telephone to ring or engaging any person in telephone conversation repeatedly or continuously with intent to annoy, abuse, or harass any person at the called number.

(6) Except as provided in section 804, the placement of telephone calls without meaningful disclosure of the caller's identity.

§ 807. False or misleading representations [15 USC 1962e]

A debt collector may not use any false, deceptive, or misleading representation or means in connection with the collection of any debt.

Without limiting the general application of the foregoing, the following conduct is a violation of this section:

(1) The false representation or implication that the debt collector is vouched for, bonded by, or affiliated with the United States or any State, including the use of any badge, uniform, or facsimile thereof.

(2) The false representation of —

(A) the character, amount, or legal status of any debt; or

(B) any services rendered or compensation which may be lawfully received by any debt collector for the collection of a debt.

(3) The false representation or implication that any individual is an attorney or that any communication is from an attorney.

(4) The representation or implication that nonpayment of any debt will result in the arrest or imprisonment of any person or the seizure, garnishment, attachment, or sale of any property or wages of any person unless such action is lawful and the debt collector or creditor intends to take such action.

(5) The threat to take any action that cannot legally be taken or that is not intended to be taken.

(6) The false representation or implication that a sale, referral, or other transfer of any interest in a debt shall cause the consumer to —

(A) Lose any claim or defense to payment of the debt; or

(B) Become subject to any practice prohibited by this title.

(7) The false representation or implication that the consumer committed any crime or other conduct in order to disgrace the consumer.

(8) Communicating or threatening to communicate to any person credit information, which is known or which should be known to be false, including the failure to communicate that, a disputed debt is disputed.

(9) The use or distribution of any written communication which simulates or is falsely represented to be a document authorized, issued, or approved by any court, official, or agency of the United States or any State, or which creates a false impression as to its source, authorization, or approval.

(10) The use of any false representation or deceptive means to collect or attempt to collect any debt or to obtain information concerning a consumer.

(11) The failure to disclose in the initial written communication with the consumer and, in addition, if the initial communication with the consumer is oral, in that initial oral communication, that the debt collector is attempting to collect a debt and that any information obtained will be used for that purpose, and the failure to disclose in subsequent communications that the communication is from a debt collector, except that this paragraph shall not apply to a formal pleading made in connection with a legal action.

(12) The false representation or implication that accounts have been turned over to innocent purchasers for value.

(13) The false representation or implication that documents are legal process.

(14) The use of any business, company, or organization name other than the true name of the debt collector's business, company, or organization.

(15) The false representation or implication that documents are not legal process forms or do not require action by the consumer.

(16) The false representation or implication that a debt collector operates or is employed by a consumer reporting agency as defined by section 603(f) of this Act.

§ 808. Unfair practices [15 USC 1692f]

A debt collector may not use unfair or unconscionable means to collect or attempt to collect any debt. Without limiting the general application of the foregoing, the following conduct is a violation of this section:

(1) The collection of any amount (including any interest, fee, charge, or expense incidental to the principal obligation) unless such amount is expressly authorized by the agreement creating the debt or permitted by law.

(2) The acceptance by a debt collector from any person of a check or other payment instrument postdated by more than five days unless such person is notified in writing of the debt collector's intent to deposit such check or instrument not more than ten nor less than three business days prior to such deposit.

(3) The solicitation by a debt collector of any postdated check or other postdated payment instrument for the purpose of threatening or instituting criminal prosecution.

(4) Depositing or threatening to deposit any postdated check or other postdated payment instrument prior to the date on such check or instrument.

(5) Causing charges to be made to any person for communications by concealment of the true propose of the communication. Such charges include, but are not limited to, collect telephone calls and telegram fees.

(6) Taking or threatening to take any nonjudicial action to effect dispossession or disablement of property if —

(A) There is no present right to possession of the property claimed as collateral through an enforceable security interest;

(B) There is no present intention to take possession of the property; or

(C) The property is exempt by law from such dispossession or disablement.

(7) Communicating with a consumer regarding a debt by post card.

(8) Using any language or symbol, other than the debt collector's address, on any envelope when communicating with a consumer by use of the mails or by telegram, except that a debt collector may use his business name if such name does not indicate that he is in the debt collection business.

§ 809. Validation of debts [15 USC 1692g]

(a) Within five days after the initial communication with a consumer in connection with the collection of any debt, a debt collector shall, unless the following information is contained in the initial communication or the consumer has paid the debt, send the consumer a written notice containing —

(1) The amount of the debt;

(2) The name of the creditor to whom the debt is owed;

(3) a statement that unless the consumer, within thirty days after receipt of the notice, disputes the validity of the debt, or any portion thereof, the debt will be assumed to be valid by the debt collector;

(4) a statement that if the consumer notifies the debt collector in writing within the thirty-day period that the debt, or any portion thereof, is disputed, the debt collector will obtain verification of the debt or a copy of a judgment against the consumer and a copy of such verification or judgment will be mailed to the consumer by the debt collector; and

(5) A statement that, upon the consumer's written request within the thirty-day period, the debt collector will provide

the consumer with the name and address of the original creditor, if different from the current creditor.

(b) If the consumer notifies the debt collector in writing within the thirty-day period described in subsection (a) that the debt, or any portion thereof, is disputed, or that the consumer requests the name and address of the original creditor, the debt collector shall cease collection of the debt, or any disputed portion thereof, until the debt collector obtains verification of the debt or any copy of a judgment, or the name and address of the original creditor, and a copy of such verification or judgment, or name and address of the original creditor, is mailed to the consumer by the debt collector.

(c) The failure of a consumer to dispute the validity of a debt under this section may not be construed by any court as an admission of liability by the consumer.

§ 810. **Multiple debts** [15 USC 1692h]

If any consumer owes multiple debts and makes any single payment to any debt collector with respect to such debts, such debt collector may not apply such payment to any debt, which is disputed by the consumer and, where applicable, shall apply such payment in accordance with the consumer's directions.

§ 811. **Legal actions by debt collectors** [15 USC 1692i]

(a) Any debt collector who brings any legal action on a debt against any consumer shall —

(1) in the case of an action to enforce an interest in real property securing the consumer's obligation, bring such action only in a judicial district or similar legal entity in which such real property is located; or

(2) in the case of an action not described in paragraph (1), bring such action only in the judicial district or similar legal entity —

(A) in which such consumer signed the contract sued upon; or

(B) in which such consumer resides at the commencement of the action.

(b) Nothing in this title shall be construed to authorize the bringing of legal actions by debt collectors.

§ 812. Furnishing certain deceptive forms [15 USC 1692j]

(a) It is unlawful to design, compile, and furnish any form knowing that such form would be used to create the false belief in a consumer that a person other than the creditor of such consumer is participating in the collection of or in an attempt to collect a debt such consumer allegedly owes such creditor, when in fact such person is not so participating.

(b) Any person who violates this section shall be liable to the same extent and in the same manner as a debt collector is liable under section 813 for failure to comply with a provision of this title.

§ 813. Civil liability [15 USC 1692k]

(a) Except as otherwise provided by this section, any debt collector who fails to comply with any provision of this title with respect to any person is liable to such person in an amount equal to the sum of —

(1) Any actual damage sustained by such person as a result of such failure;

(2) (A) in the case of any action by an individual, such additional damages as the court may allow, but not exceeding $1,000; or

(B) in the case of a class action, (i) such amount for each named plaintiff as could be recovered under subparagraph (A), and (ii) such amount as the court may allow for all other class members, without regard to a minimum individual recovery, not to exceed the lesser of $500,000 or 1 per centum of the net worth of the debt collector; and

(3) in the case of any successful action to enforce the foregoing liability, the costs of the action, together with a reasonable attorney's fee as determined by the court. On a finding by the court that an action under this section was

brought in bad faith and for the purpose of harassment, the court may award to the defendant attorney's fees reasonable in relation to the work expended and costs.

(b) In determining the amount of liability in any action under subsection (a), the court shall consider, among other relevant factors —

(1) in any individual action under subsection (a)(2)(A), the frequency and persistence of noncompliance by the debt collector, the nature of such noncompliance, and the extent to which such noncompliance was intentional; or

(2) in any class action under subsection (a)(2)(B), the frequency and persistence of noncompliance by the debt collector, the nature of such noncompliance, the resources of the debt collector, the number of persons adversely affected, and the extent to which the debt collector's noncompliance was intentional.

(c) A debt collector may not be held liable in any action brought under this title if the debt collector shows by a preponderance of evidence that the violation was not intentional and resulted from a bona fide error notwithstanding the maintenance of procedures reasonably adapted to avoid any such error.

(d) An action to enforce any liability created by this title may be brought in any appropriate United States district court without regard to the amount in controversy, or in any other court of competent jurisdiction, within one year from the date on which the violation occurs.

(e) No provision of this section imposing any liability shall apply to any act done or omitted in good faith in conformity with any advisory opinion of the Commission, notwithstanding that after such act or omission has occurred, such opinion is amended, rescinded, or determined by judicial or other authority to be invalid for any reason.

§ 814. Administrative enforcement [15 USC 1692*l*]

(a) Compliance with this title shall be enforced by the Commission, except to the extend that enforcement of the requirements imposed under this title is specifically committed to another agency under subsection (b). For purpose of the exercise by the Commission of its functions and powers under the Federal Trade Commission Act, a violation of this title shall be deemed an unfair or deceptive act or practice in violation of that Act. All of the functions and powers of the Commission under the Federal Trade Commission Act are available to the Commission to enforce compliance by any person with this title, irrespective of whether that person is engaged in commerce or meets any other jurisdictional tests in the Federal Trade Commission Act, including the power to enforce the provisions of this title in the same manner as if the violation had been a violation of a Federal Trade Commission trade regulation rule.

(b) Compliance with any requirements imposed under this title shall be enforced under —

(1) Section 8 of the Federal Deposit Insurance Act, in the case of —

(A) National banks, by the Comptroller of the Currency;

(B) Member banks of the Federal Reserve System (other than national banks), by the Federal Reserve Board; and

(C) Banks the deposits or accounts of which are insured by the Federal Deposit Insurance Corporation (other than members of the Federal Reserve System), by the Board of Directors of the Federal Deposit Insurance Corporation;

(2) Section 5(d) of the Home Owners Loan Act of 1933, section 407 of the National Housing Act, and sections 6(i) and 17 of the Federal Home Loan Bank Act, by the Federal Home Loan Bank Board (acting directing or through the Federal Savings and Loan Insurance Corporation), in the case of any institution subject to any of those provisions;

(3) The Federal Credit Union Act, by the Administrator of the National Credit Union Administration with respect to any Federal credit union;

(4) Subtitle IV of Title 49, by the Interstate Commerce Commission with respect to any common carrier subject to such subtitle;

(5) The Federal Aviation Act of 1958, by the Secretary of Transportation with respect to any air carrier or any foreign air carrier subject to that Act; and

(6) The Packers and Stockyards Act, 1921 (except as provided in section 406 of that Act), by the Secretary of Agriculture with respect to any activities subject to that Act.

(c) For the purpose of the exercise by any agency referred to in subsection (b) of its powers under any Act referred to in that subsection, a violation of any requirement imposed under this title shall be deemed to be a violation of a requirement imposed under that Act. In addition to its powers under any provision of law specifically referred to in subsection (b), each of the agencies referred to in that subsection may exercise, for the purpose of enforcing compliance with any requirement imposed under this title any other authority conferred on it by law, except as provided in subsection (d).

(d) Neither the Commission nor any other agency referred to in subsection (b) may promulgate trade regulation rules or other regulations with respect to the collection of debts by debt collectors as defined in this title.

§ 815. Reports to Congress by the Commission [15 USC 1692m]

(a) Not later than one year after the effective date of this title and at one-year intervals thereafter, the Commission shall make reports to the Congress concerning the administration of its functions under this title, including such recommendations as the Commission deems necessary or appropriate. In addition, each report of the Commission shall include its assessment of the extent to which compliance with this title is being achieved and a summary of the enforcement actions taken by the Commission under section 814 of this title.

(b) In the exercise of its functions under this title, the Commission may obtain upon request the views of any other Federal agency, which exercises enforcement functions under section 814 of this title.

§ 816. Relation to State laws [15 USC 1692n]

This title does not annul, alter, or affect, or exempt any person subject to the provisions of this title from complying with the laws of any State with respect to debt collection practices, except to the extent that those laws are inconsistent with any provision of this title, and then only to the extent of the inconsistency. For purposes of this section, a State law is not inconsistent with this title if the protection such law affords any consumer is greater than the protection provided by this title.

§ 817. Exemption for State regulation [15 USC 1692o]

The Commission shall by regulation exempt from the requirements of this title any class of debt collection practices within any State if the Commission determines that under the law of that State that class of debt collection practices is subject to requirements substantially similar to those imposed by this title, and that there is adequate provision for enforcement.

§ 818. Effective date [15 USC 1692 note]

This title takes effect upon the expiration of six months after the date of its enactment, but section 809 shall apply only with respect to debts for which the initial attempt to collect occurs after such effective date.
Approved September 20, 1977

Lonnie R. Mathews

ENDNOTES
1. So in original; however, should read "604(a)(3)."

LEGISLATIVE HISTORY:

Public Law 95-109 [H.R. 5294]
HOUSE REPORT No. 95-131 (Comm. on Banking, Finance, and Urban Affairs).
SENATE REPORT No. 95-382 (Comm. on Banking, Housing, and Urban Affairs).
CONGRESSIONAL RECORD, Vol. 123 (1977):

Apr. 4, considered and passed House.

Aug. 5, considered and passed Senate, amended.

Sept. 8, House agreed to Senate amendment.

WEEKLY COMPILATION OF PRESIDENTIAL DOCUMENTS, Vol. 13, No. 39:

Sept. 20, Presidential statement.

AMENDMENTS:

SECTION 621, SUBSECTIONS (b)(3), (b)(4) and (b)(5) were amended to transfer certain administrative enforcement responsibilities, pursuant to Pub. L. 95-473, § 3(b), Oct. 17, 1978. 92 Stat. 166; Pub. L. 95-630, Title V. § 501, November 10, 1978, 92 Stat. 3680; Pub. L. 98-443, § 9(h), Oct. 4, 1984, 98 Stat. 708.

SECTION 803, SUBSECTION (6), defining "debt collector," was amended to repeal the attorney at law exemption at former Section (6)(F) and to redesignate Section 803(6)(G) pursuant to Pub. L. 99-361, July 9, 1986, 100 Stat. 768. For legislative history, *see* H.R. 237, HOUSE REPORT No. 99-405 (Comm. on Banking, Finance and Urban Affairs). CONGRESSIONAL RECORD: Vol. 131 (1985): Dec. 2, considered and passed House. Vol. 132 (1986): June 26, considered and passed Senate.

SECTION 807, SUBSECTION (11), was amended to affect when debt collectors must state (a) that they are attempting to collect a debt and (b) that information obtained will be used for that purpose, pursuant to Pub. L. 104-208 § 2305, 110 Stat. 3009 (Sept. 30, 1996).

Fair Credit Reporting

If you've ever applied for a charge account, a personal loan, insurance, or a job, there's a file about you. This file contains information on where you work and live, how you pay your bills, and whether you've been sued, arrested, or filed for bankruptcy.

Companies that gather and sell this information are called Consumer Reporting Agencies (CRAs). The most common type of CRA is the credit bureau. The information CRAs sell about you to creditors, employers, insurers, and other businesses is called a consumer report.

The Fair Credit Reporting Act (FCRA), enforced by the Federal Trade Commission, is designed to promote accuracy and ensure the privacy of the information used in consumer reports. Recent amendments to the Act expand your rights and place additional requirements on CRAs. Businesses that supply information about you to CRAs and those that use consumer reports also have new responsibilities under the law.

Here are some questions consumers commonly ask about consumer reports and CRAs - and the answers. Note that you may have additional rights under state laws. Contact your state Attorney General or local consumer protection agency for more information.

Q. How do I find the CRA that has my report?

A. Contact the CRAs listed in the Yellow Pages under "credit" or "credit rating and reporting." Because more than one CRA may have a file on you, call each until you locate all the agencies maintaining your file. The three major national credit bureaus are:

Equifax
800-685-1111
www.equifax.com

Experian
888-EXPERIAN (888-397-3742)
www.experian.com

Trans Union
800-916-8800
www.transunion.com

In addition, anyone who takes action against you in response to a report supplied by a CRA - such as denying your application for credit, insurance, or employment - must give you the name, address, and telephone number of the CRA that provided the report.

. Do I have a right to know what's in my report?

A. Yes, if you ask for it. The CRA must tell you everything in your report, including medical information, and in most cases, the sources of the information. The CRA also must give you a list of everyone who has requested your report within the past year - two years for employment related requests.

Q. Is there a charge for my report?

A. Sometimes. There's no charge if a company takes adverse action against you, such as denying your application for credit, insurance or employment, and you request your report within 60 days of receiving the notice of the action. The notice will give you the name, address, and phone number of the CRA. In addition, you're entitled to one free report a year (1) you're unemployed and plan to look for a job within 60 days, (2) you're on welfare, or (3) your report is inaccurate because of fraud. Otherwise, a CRA may charge you up to $9 for a copy of your report.

Q. What can I do about inaccurate or incomplete information?

A. Under the new law, both the CRA and the information provider have responsibilities for correcting inaccurate or incomplete information in your report. To protect all your rights under this law, contact both the CRA and the information provider.

First, tell the CRA in writing what information you believe is inaccurate. CRAs must reinvestigate the items in question - usually within 30 days - unless they consider your dispute frivolous. They also must forward all relevant data you provide about the dispute to the information provider. After the information provider receives notice of a dispute from the CRA, it must investigate, review all relevant information provided by the CRA, and report the results to the CRA. If the information provider finds the disputed information to be inaccurate, it must notify all nationwide CRAs so that they can correct this information in your file.

When the reinvestigation is complete, the CRA must give you the written results and a free copy of your report if the dispute results in a change. If an item is changed or removed, the CRA cannot put the disputed information back in your file unless the information provider verifies its accuracy and completeness, and the CRA gives you a written notice that includes the name, address, and phone number of the provider.

Second, tell the creditor or other information provider in writing that you dispute an item. Many providers specify an address for disputes. If the provider then reports the item to any CRA, it must include a notice of your dispute. In addition, if you are correct - that is, if the information is inaccurate - the information provider may not use it again.

Q. What can I do if the CRA or information provider won't correct the information I dispute?

A. A reinvestigation may not resolve your dispute with the CRA. If that's the case, ask the CRA to include your statement of the dispute in your file and in future reports. If you request, the CRA also will provide your statement to anyone who received a copy of the old report in the recent past. There usually is a fee for this service.

If you tell the information provider that you dispute an item, a notice of your dispute must be included anytime the information provider reports the item to a CRA.

Q. Can my employer get my report?

A. Only if you say it's okay. A CRA may not supply information about you to your employer, or to a prospective employer, without your consent.

Q. Can creditors, employers, or insurers get a report that contains medical information about me?

A. Not without your approval.

Q. What should I know about "investigative consumer reports"?

A. "Investigative consumer reports" are detailed reports that involve interviews with your neighbors or acquaintances about your lifestyle, character, and reputation. They may be used in connection with insurance and employment applications. You'll be notified in writing when a company orders such a report. The notice will explain your right to request certain information about the report from the company you applied to. If your application is rejected, you may get additional information from the CRA. However, the CRA does not have to reveal the sources of the information.

Q. How long can a CRA report negative information?

A. Seven years. There are certain exceptions:

- Information about criminal convictions may be reported without any time limitation.

- Bankruptcy information may be reported for 10 years.

- Information reported in response to an application for a job with a salary of more than $75,000 has no time limit.

- Information reported because of an application for more than $150,000 worth of credit or life insurance has no time limit.

- Information about a lawsuit or an unpaid judgment against you can be reported for seven years or until the statute of limitations runs out, whichever is longer.

Q. Can anyone get a copy of my report?

A. No. Only people with a legitimate business need, as recognized by the FCRA. For example, a company is allowed to get your report if you apply for credit, insurance, employment, or to rent an apartment.

Q. How can I stop a CRA from including me on lists for unsolicited credit and insurance offers?

A. Creditors and insurers may use CRA file information as a basis for sending you unsolicited offers. These offers must include a toll-free number for you to call if you want to remove your name and address from lists for two years; completing a form that the CRA provides for this purpose will keep your name off the lists permanently.

Q. Do I have the right to sue for damages?

A. You may sue a CRA, a user or - in some cases - a provider of CRA data, in state or federal court for most violations of the FCRA. If you win, the defendant will have to pay damages and reimburse you for attorney fees to the extent ordered by the court.

Q. Are there other laws I should know about?

A. Yes. If your credit application was denied, the Equal Credit Opportunity Act requires creditors to specify why - if you ask. For example, the creditor must tell you whether you were denied because you have "no credit file" with a CRA or because the CRA says you have "delinquent obligations." The ECOA also requires creditors to consider additional information you might supply about your credit history. You may want to find out why the creditor denied your application before you contact the CRA.

Q. Where should I report violations of the law?

A. Although the FTC can't act as your lawyer in private disputes, information about your experiences and concerns is vital to the enforcement of the Fair Credit Reporting Act. Send your questions or complaints to: Consumer Response Center - FCRA, Federal Trade Commission, Washington, DC 20580.

About Alliance Financial Ministries, Inc.

Alliance Financial Ministries is a non-profit Christian debt management company dedicated to helping individuals establish financial freedom. Unlike most debt management firms Alliance financial works with **YOU** the consumer and NOT the creditors. At Alliance we help our clients design a workable plan to reduce, and ultimately eliminate, their debt.

We not only treat the symptom of being in debt, but also focus on the true problem—which in most cases it is the lack of *Discipline, Self-control,* and *Commitment* that leads to debt in the first place. It is our belief that not knowing how you fell into debt will inevitably lead to repeating the mistakes that caused the debt in the first place.

Alliance Financial Ministries provides counseling to assist families, who are in financial turmoil at no charge. We offer one-on-one Christian counseling, using God's principles of money management. Our goal is to give you the client, a sensible plan to make a sincere and honest effort to repay creditors at the lowest cost and the shortest time possible.

FINANCIAL FREEDOM

Let no debt remain outstanding, except the continuing debt to love one another, for he who loves his fellowman has fulfilled the law. –Romans 13:8

Our financial freedom plan is a multi-step process, which involves the following:

- **Make a decision to operate 100 percent on cash.**

  That means once you have made the decision to change your life you must not use debt of any kind while in the process of gaining financial freedom. You and your entire family must be totally committed to become debt free, and live completely on cash.

- **Develop a Spending Plan**

  You and only you must take responsibility for your financial situation. Stop using excuses and being the victim; take charge of your finances. A major step in taking charge of your finances is to sit down and develop a plan. Nothing can be gained financially if you don't have a clue as to where your money is going; this step involves knowing exactly what your income is spent on. Our counselors will assist in preparing a detailed budget based upon your income and living expenses. They also provide the needed guidance to ensure a commitment to financial freedom.

  Traditionally, a budget has negative connotations associated with it. However a budget is the exact opposite. First, think of a budget as a spending plan where you are deciding what you are going to spend your income on before you receive it. *YOU* make the choice where your money is spent based on the priorities *YOU* set.

If financial freedom is your priority then every dollar that you have after your basic needs have been met should go towards debt reduction. We have come to realize that over time your real priorities will surface and the less important desires will fade.

Bibliography

Every effort has been made to give complete bibliographic information for all references if the reader desires more specific information regarding any source; he or she should contact the authors.

"Financial Peace" *Dave Ramsey Viking Press 1996*

"Your finance in changing times" *Larry Burkett Moody press 1975*

"Using your money wisely" *Larry Burkett Moody press 1985*

"God's plans for your finances" *Dwight Nichols Whitaker House 1998*

"Debt-free & Prosperous living" *John Cummuta 1998*

"Your money counts" *Howard Dayton Crown - financial ministries, 1996*

BIOGRAPHY Lonnie R. Mathews

Lonnie R. Mathews is a native of Birmingham, Alabama, and shortly after high school Lonnie joined the United States Marine Corps. He successfully served eight years in the Corps, and is a veteran of Desert Shield and Desert Storm. Lonnie was honorably discharged on December 2, 1992, and enrolled at the University of Alabama Tuscaloosa where he graduated with a Bachelor of Science degree in *Finance and Investment management.* Lonnie is married to Carrie with a daughter Corrie and currently resides in Pearland, Texas. Lonnie and Carrie are members of New Hope Baptist Church in Clute, Texas.

Prior to founding Alliance Financial Ministries, Inc, Lonnie worked in several areas of the financial services industry. Working as an analyst in the corporate loans division of Wachovia Bank of Georgia, he gained valuable experience in banking and learned how banks use cash. Lonnie's main function was to analyze major corporations who wished to borrow several million dollars from the bank. Not satisfied with this position, Lonnie relocated to the Houston area in 1997 where he began his career in the financial services industry. Lonnie worked for three years with a major New York stock exchange brokerage firm as a financial planner before becoming an independent agent.

Being in debt most of his adult life, Lonnie and his wife realized that this was not God's plan for their finances. After much prayer and seeking God in their finances, it became clear that being in debt was not the answer. As a result of his new found freedom and financial peace Lonnie Co-founded Alliance Financial Ministries, Inc. The goal of this ministry is to help individuals understand a biblically based philosophy of money management. Lonnie currently conducts financial seminars and teaches classes at churches nationally.

Printed in the United States
26036LVS00003B/530